T0390057

SUNISA LEE

BY GOLRIZ GOLKAR

TORQUE™

BELLWETHER MEDIA · MINNEAPOLIS, MN

Torque brims with excitement perfect for thrill-seekers of all kinds. Discover daring survival skills, explore uncharted worlds, and marvel at mighty engines and extreme sports. In *Torque* books, anything can happen. Are you ready?

This edition first published in 2025 by Bellwether Media, Inc.

Library of Congress Cataloging-in-Publication Data

Names: Golkar, Golriz, author.
Title: Sunisa Lee / by Golriz Golkar.
Description: Minneapolis, MN : Bellwether Media, 2025. | Series: Sports superstars | Includes bibliographical references and index. | Audience: Ages 7-12 | Audience: Grades 4-6 | Summary: "Engaging images accompany information about Sunisa Lee. The combination of high-interest subject matter and light text is intended for students in grades 3 through 7"– Provided by publisher.
Identifiers: LCCN 2024010417 (print) | LCCN 2024010418 (ebook) | ISBN 9798893040388 (library binding) | ISBN 9781644879788 (ebook)
Subjects: LCSH: Lee, Sunisa, 2003–Juvenile literature. | Women gymnasts–United States–Biography–Juvenile literature. | Women Olympic athletes–United States–Biography–Juvenile literature.
Classification: LCC GV460.2.L44 G65 2025 (print) | LCC GV460.2.L44 (ebook) | DDC 796.44092 [B]–dc23/eng/20240307
LC record available at https://lccn.loc.gov/2024010417
LC ebook record available at https://lccn.loc.gov/2024010418

Editor: Kieran Downs   Designer: Gabriel Hilger

Printed in the United States of America, North Mankato, MN.

TABLE OF CONTENTS

GOING FOR GOLD

It is the 2019 U.S. National **Championships**. Sunisa Lee is **competing** on the **uneven bars**. She leaps into the air and grabs the bar. She flips and twists her body. Then she leaps to the other bar.

Lee flies through the air again. She flips. She lands on her feet. Lee wins the gold medal!

MAKING HISTORY

LEE IS THE FIRST HMONG AMERICAN TO COMPETE ON THE U.S. WOMEN'S GYMNASTICS TEAM.

WHO IS SUNISA LEE?

Sunisa Lee is a **gymnast**. She has won **Olympic** medals and championship titles. She is known for her skills on the uneven bars.

Brand Partner

Lee appears in ads for many companies. They include Target, Gatorade, Clif Bars, and Amazon.

SUNISA LEE

BIRTHDAY	March 9, 2003
HOMETOWN	Saint Paul, Minnesota
EVENTS	all-around, balance beam, floor exercise, uneven bars, vault
HEIGHT	5 feet
JOINED	U.S. Junior National Team in 2017

Lee also supports **charities**. She helps raise money for children's education and sports programs. She also works to help women in sports.

A RISING STAR

Lee loved gymnastics as a child. She practiced on a **balance beam** in her yard. She started officially training at age 6. Lee was a standout. A coach helped her train for the USA Gymnastics Junior Olympic program.

LEE ON BALANCE BEAM

Lee learned new skills. In 2014, she was named an **elite** gymnast. Lee was only 11 years old.

Lee joined the U.S. Junior National Team in 2017. They competed at the Gymnix International Junior Cup that year. Lee won silver in the uneven bars. She helped her team win a gold medal.

In 2018, Lee won gold in the uneven bars at the U.S. National Championships. She also helped her team win gold at the Pacific Rim Championships.

KEEPING HER BALANCE

LEE'S FAVORITE EVENT IS THE BALANCE BEAM.

FAVORITES

BOOK SERIES	MOVIE	FOOD	HOBBY

 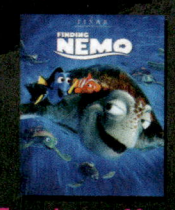  

| Harry Potter | Finding Nemo | pasta | camping |

11

MAKING HISTORY

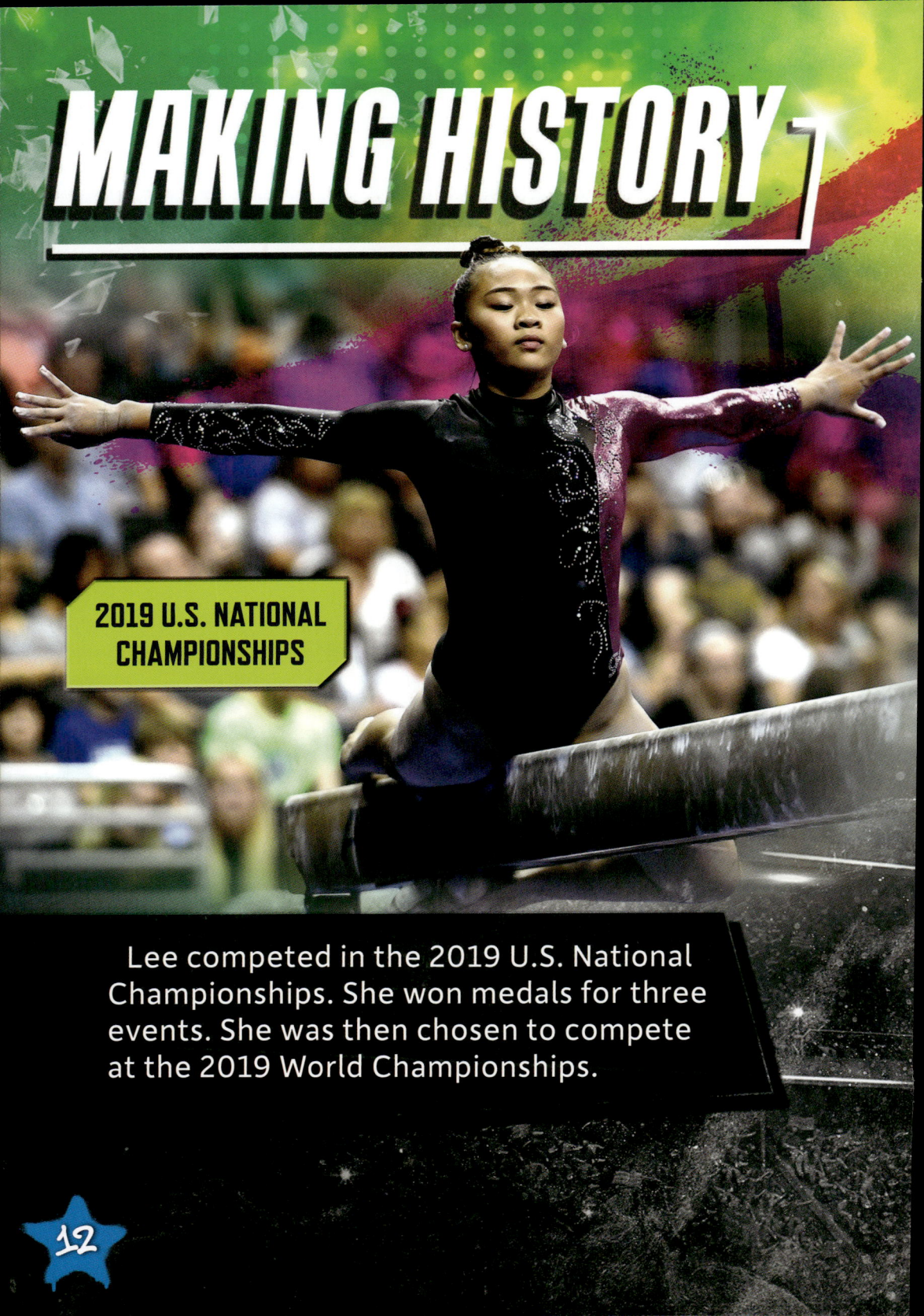

Lee competed in the 2019 U.S. National Championships. She won medals for three events. She was then chosen to compete at the 2019 World Championships.

At the World Championships, Lee won a silver medal for the **floor exercise**. She also won a bronze medal for the uneven bars. Lee helped the U.S. women's team win a gold medal.

2019 WORLD CHAMPIONSHIPS

13

Many gyms closed in 2020 due to **COVID-19**. Lee could not train. Then she hurt her ankle. She did not practice for months.

But Lee never gave up. She competed in the 2021 U.S. National Championships. Lee won gold for the uneven bars. She also took home silver medals in the **all-around** and balance beam events.

2021 U.S. NATIONAL CHAMPIONSHIPS

TROPHY SHELF

1 Olympic gold medal

1 Olympic silver medal

1 Olympic bronze medal

In 2021, Lee won a spot on the U.S. Women's Gymnastics team. She competed at the Tokyo Olympic Games that summer.

Lee won a bronze medal in the uneven bars. She also won a team silver medal. But Lee's biggest win was the all-around gold medal!

SUNISA LEE MAP

⊙ 2020 Tokyo Olympic Games, Tokyo, Japan

AMERICAN PRIDE

LEE'S ALL-AROUND GOLD WAS THE FIFTH IN A ROW FOR AMERICAN FEMALE GYMNASTS.

17

Lee went to Auburn University after the Olympic Games. She joined the gymnastics team. In 2022, she won the balance beam event at the **NCAA** Championships. She also finished second in the all-around.

Lee became one of the top-ranked NCAA gymnasts. But she decided to leave college in 2023. She wanted to return to **professional** gymnastics.

TIMELINE

— 2014 —
Lee becomes an elite gymnast

— 2017 —
Lee joins the U.S. Junior National Team

— 2019 —
Lee wins three medals at the World Championships

18

2022 NCAA CHAMPIONSHIPS

STEVENS · URNE · WATSON

— 2021 —
Lee wins three
medals at the
Tokyo Olympic
Games

— 2021 —
Lee goes
to Auburn
University

— 2023 —
Lee leaves college
to train for the
2024 Paris
Olympic Games

19

LEE'S FUTURE

Lee works with companies that support women's sports. They help give all women access to sports training.

DANCER

In 2021, Lee competed on the show *Dancing with the Stars*. She placed fifth.

Health problems have made it hard for Lee to compete. But she still plans to compete in the 2024 Paris Olympic Games. Lee continues to train hard!

GLOSSARY

all-around—a category of gymnastics that includes all of the events; the all-around champion earns the highest total score from all events put together.

balance beam—a long beam that is raised in the air

championships—contests to decide the best team or person

charities—organizations that help others in need

competing—working for something for which another person is also working

COVID-19—a virus that led to shutdowns and millions of deaths around the world

elite—related to a level in gymnastics that lets a gymnast compete in national and international competitions

floor exercise—a gymnastics event in which movements are performed on the floor in a special area

gymnast—a person who competes in gymnastics; gymnastics is a sport in which competitors perform moves that show their balance and strength.

NCAA—National Collegiate Athletic Association; the NCAA is in charge of student athletes at colleges in the United States.

Olympic—related to a worldwide summer or winter sports contest held in a different country every four years

professional—related to a player, team, or coach who makes money from a sport

uneven bars—a gymnastics event in which gymnasts do moves in between a pair of bars set at different heights

TO LEARN MORE

AT THE LIBRARY

Fishman, Jon M. *Suni Lee*. Minneapolis, Minn.: Lerner Publications, 2022.

Lawrence, Blythe. *Trailblazing Women in Gymnastics*. Chicago, Ill.: Norwood House Press, 2023.

Martinson, Morgan. *Suni Lee*. North Mankato, Minn.: Abdo Publishing, 2022.

ON THE WEB

FACTSURFER

Factsurfer.com gives you a safe, fun way to find more information.

1. Go to www.factsurfer.com

2. Enter "Sunisa Lee" into the search box and click 🔍.

3. Select your book cover to see a list of related content.

INDEX